OUTLINES ON REVELATION

Croft M. Pentz

BAKER BOOK HOUSE
Grand Rapids, Michigan

To **Reverend George Hatchner**
in appreciation for his service
and kindness to the Pentz family.

First printing, April 1978
Second printing, March 1980
Third printing, December 1981
Fourth printing, November 1982
Fifth printing, February 1984
Sixth printing, November 1985
Seventh printing, October 1987

Copyright 1978
by Baker Book House Company
ISBN: 0-8010-7030-9

Printed in the United States of America

CONTENTS

FOREWORD

Selecting themes for sermons is not always an easy task. Even those who are able to give all their time to reading and studying are sometimes glad of a suggestion by which they are directed to a certain topic.

After close examination of these sermon outlines, I am sure that teachers and pastors will find them most beneficial in their labor of love.

We cannot do less than express our gratitude to the compiler of these sermon outlines. I am certain that if these outlines are used prayerfully, they will touch the hearts of multitudes of people. May God richly bless these sermons as they go forth.

—Pastor Robert C. Porter
Community Free Will Baptist Church
Westland, Michigan

PREFACE

During the first twenty-two years of my ministry I prepared and had published, sermon outlines on each book of the New Testament—except the Book of Revelation.

When a number of minister friends suggested that I outline Revelation, I at first declined, as I knew there were many conflicting viewpoints on the book. Finally in 1973, with fear and trembling, I accepted their challenge.

I have tried not to be dogmatic. Some readers will disagree with my viewpoints on many events in Revelation, however, as Christians we can disagree and still be friends.

In no way do I intend for these outlines to be a commentary. Nor do I set myself up as an authority on prophecy. With these outlines, I suggest reliable commentaries, and other reference books.

My thanks to the people of my church who received these sermons as I delivered them, to my typist Mrs. Ella Steinbach, and to Pastor Robert Porter for the foreword.

I trust these outlines will be a blessing to fellow Christian workers. May we do all we can to prepare men for that great event—the Second Coming of Christ.

—Croft M. Pentz

INTRODUCTORY INFORMATION

The Book of Revelation is perhaps the most misunderstood book of the Bible. Yet, there may be more books written on it than any other.

The word *revelation* means to "open," "unveil," or "make simple so all understand." The Book of Revelation is often called the Apocalypse.

Note these verses: ". . . blessed is he that keepeth the sayings of the prophecy of this book" (Rev. 22:7); "Blessed is he that readeth, and they that hear the words of this prophecy, and keep those things which are written therein: for the time is at hand" (Rev. 1:3).

God wants us to understand this book. "Seal not the sayings of the prophecy of this book: for the time is at hand" (Rev. 22:10). "He that hath an ear, let him hear what the Spirit saith," appears seven times.

Passages in Revelation also appear in these Old Testament books: Isaiah, Daniel, Joel, and Zechariah.

The number *seven* appears often in Revelation. For example:

1) Seven churches
2) Seven seals
3) Seven trumpets
4) Seven signs
5) Seven vials
6) Seven-fold judgment
7) Seven-fold triumph

Dr. Griffith Thomas has outlined the Bible this way:

Genesis to Deuteronomy—Revelation
Joshua to Esther—Preparation
Job to Song of Solomon—Aspiration
Isaiah to Malachi—Expectation
Matthew to John—Manifestation
Acts to Jude—Realization
The Apocalypse—Consummation

Dr. W. Graham Scroggie, in *The Unfolding Drama of Redemption,* outlined Revelation:
Revelation 1: The Christ
Revelation 2–3: The Church
Revelation 4–22: The Consummation

Note the comparison of Genesis and Revelation by Scroggie:

GENESIS	REVELATION
God	God
First heaven and earth	Last heaven and earth
First rest	Final rest
Paradise lost	Paradise regained
The tree and the river	The tree and the river
Husband and wife	The Lamb and the bride

Note the contrast of Genesis and Revelation by Scroggie:

GENESIS	REVELATION
Satan victorious	Satan defeated
Judgment pronounced	Judgment executed
The divine face hidden	We shall see His face
The curse pronounced	The cursed removed
The gates are shut against us	The gates are never shut
Death overtook all men	There is no more death
All faces wet with tears	All tears wiped away
Terror came with the night	No terror because there is no night
Banished from the tree of life	We have a right to the tree of life
Exiles from the earthly garden	Inheritors of the heavenly city
The cherubim keeping man out	The cherubim welcoming man in

Three views of the coming of Christ:
1. Posttribulation. The church will be raptured after the seven-year tribulation.
2. Midtribulation. The church will be raptured after three and one-half years of the tribulation (at the middle of the tribulation).
3. Pretribulation. The church will be raptured before the tribulation and saved from all tribulation. These people believe Christ may return at any time.

(The word *rapture* does not appear in the Bible. Rapture means a "catching away" of Christians to be with the Lord. Also note a difference between persecution and tribulation. Persecution comes from man, but tribulation is the punishment of God toward man.)

Salem Kirban gives the stages of the earth in his *Prophetic Charts*.
1. Original earth—Genesis 1:1
2. Earth cursed (man's sins)—Genesis 3
3. Antedeluvian (before the flood) Age (wickedness increases)—II Peter 2:5
4. Flood judgment—Genesis 7:4
5. Present evil age—Galatians 1:4
6. Tribulation period judgment—Zechariah 14:3, 4
7. 1,000 year millennial age—Revelation 20:4
8. Earth destroyed by fire—II Peter 3:10
9. The new heavens and new earth—Revelation 21:1

1

THE SPEAKING CHRIST
Revelation 1:1-11

During the time that the apostle John was exiled on the isle of Patmos, he received a vision from God concerning the events of the endtime. Because many symbols are used throughout the Book of Revelation, we must remember to use Scripture to interpret Scripture. We must keep in mind that "no prophecy of the scripture is of any private interpretation" (II Peter 1:20).

I. THE PURPOSE—vv. 1-3
    A. Revelation. "The Revelation of Jesus Christ."
    B. Reason. "Things which must shortly come to pass."
       1. Rapture
       2. Tribulation
       3. Millennium
       4. New heaven
       5. New earth
    C. Revealing. "And he sent and signified it by his angel unto his servant John."
    D. Record—v. 2. John recorded:
       1. The word of God
       2. The testimony of Jesus
       3. All things he saw
    E. Respect—v. 3. A blessing is given to:
       1. Those who read the book
       2. Those who hear the words of the prophecy
       3. Those who keep the words of the book

II. THE PEOPLE—vv. 4-6
    A. Churches—v. 4. The message was given from Christ to the seven churches in Turkey and to John. John who was one of the disciples, wrote

13

the Gospel of John and the three Epistles of John.

B. Christ—v. 5
1. Person. Jesus is:
   a. The faithful witness
   b. The first begotten of the dead
   c. The prince of the kings of the earth
2. Pardon. Jesus loved us and washed away our sins in His blood. (See I John 1:7; I Peter 1:19.)

C. Christians—v. 6. Christ has made us (Christians) kings and priests unto God.

III. THE PERSON—vv. 7-8
A. His coming—v. 7. When He comes, every eye shall see Him (cf. I Thess. 4:13-18).
B. His character—v. 8. The Alpha and Omega are the first and last letters of the Greek alphabet. Christ had no beginning and will have no ending. Christ was with God at creation (Gen. 1:26). John said all things were made by Christ (John 1:3; cf. Col. 1:16-17).

IV. THE PROPHECY—vv. 9-11
A. Companion—v. 9. John is our brother and companion. John was exiled to the isle of Patmos for the sake of the gospel.
B. Communion—v. 10. John was "in the Spirit" or simply in touch with God. He heard the voice of God. When we are in touch with God, He will speak to us (Isa. 6:1-8).
C. Churches—v. 11. God commanded John to write what He had to say to the seven churches.

Though God was speaking to John on the isle of Patmos, He was speaking to all mankind through John. God still speaks to men today. However, if men expect God to speak to them, they must be open and receptive and live close to God.

2

THE APPEARANCE OF CHRIST
Revelation 1:12-20

God has always revealed Himself to those who seek Him. John was with Christ for three years. Christ revealed the future to him, so that John could share it with others.

I. THE CHRIST—vv. 12-16
    A. Symbol—v. 12. John sees the seven golden candlesticks which represent the seven churches.
    B. Savior—vv. 13-16. Christ stands in the midst of the candlesticks.
        1. Christ—v. 13. Christ stands near those who follow Him, and even near those who disobey Him. He stands near by to woo the lost back.
        2. Characteristic—14-16. Descriptions here are from Daniel 9:9, 13; 10:5, 6; Ezekiel 1:24. These Scriptures show Christ's omnipotence and judgment. He appears also in Revelation 14:14 as the Son of Man and in Daniel 7:13.

II. THE CHARACTERISTICS OF CHRIST—vv. 17-18
    A. Honor. "And when I saw him, I fell at his feet as dead." All men must someday bow before Him (Phil. 2:9-11).
    B. Help. "Fear not; I am the first and last." His message has always been "fear not." He is the "first and last"—the eternal God.

C. Hope. "I am He that liveth, and was dead; and behold, I am alive for evermore." In John 3:16; 11:25-27, Jesus spoke of His eternal existence.

D. Holding. "And have the keys of hell and of death." Jesus has all authority. (See Matthew 16:16-19.)

III. THE CONTENT—v. 19

Note the three-fold command to John:

A. Write the things which thou has seen—past
B. Write the things which are—present
C. Write the things which shall be hereafter—future

Keep in mind that all Scripture is given by inspiration of God (II Tim. 3:16). Also remember that God's Word shall never pass away (Matt. 24:35).

IV. THE CHURCHES—v. 20

A. The mystery. "The mystery of the seven stars which thou sawest in my right hand, and the seven golden candlesticks." Although John calls this a *mystery*, God wants us to understand His Word.

B. The meaning:
1. The seven stars are the angels of the seven churches.
2. The seven candlesticks which John saw are the seven churches.

C. Appearance of Christ. He may not appear to us in a vision as He did for John, however we can see Him other ways.
1. Through the Scriptures
2. When we pray (see Isaiah 40:31, waiting before the Lord).
3. When we attend His house

3

THE EPHESUS CHURCH
Revelation 2:1-7

God knows all about His people. He knows about men's sins, shortcomings, and slothfulness. Because He knows all about men, God does everything in His power to help change them. But since men have wills, it is up to them to make the choice to change. God constantly helps men draw near to Himself, knowing that He is the only answer to their problems.

I. **THE CHURCH**—v. 1
   A. The church of Ephesus was located in a commercial center where at one of the ancient wonders, the Temple of Diana, the goddess Diana was worshiped (Acts 19:27).
   B. Christ. He walked in the midst of the candlesticks. The rightful place for Christ is in the midst of His church, however, He must be welcomed there (Rev. 3:20).

II. **THE CONCERN**—vv. 2-3
   A. Purity—v. 2. Christ knew all about these people.
      1. Their work
      2. Their patience
      3. Their purity
         a. Christ wants His church to be pure (Eph. 5:27).
         b. Purity is a personal matter (II Cor. 7:1). Only the Lord has the power to cleanse, yet only man has the choice of allowing God to cleanse him.
   B. Patience—v. 3. They were patient and faithful as God wants men to be (Rev. 2:10). All He asks of men is to follow Him, and He will

"make them" what He wants them to be. Two of the most needed virtues are patience and faithfulness.

III. **THE COMPLAINT**—vv. 4-6
   A. Reckless—v. 4. The people were reckless and were becoming indifferent. As the result, they lost their first love—their love for God. No one can fully love others until they love God. (Note the words of Jesus in Matthew 22:37.) After we love Him, we will then love others as we love ourselves (Matt. 22:39).
   B. Repentance—v. 5.
      1. Remember. From where thou art fallen.
      2. Repent. Repent and do the first works.
      3. Removal. If you do not repent, Christ will remove your candlestick.
   C. Remembrance—v. 6. Remember the wicked deeds of Nicolaitans. He taught fornication and adultery as not being sin.

IV. **THE COMPENSATION**—v. 7
   A. Hearing. "He that hath an ear, let him hear what the Spirit saith unto the churches." We are not to be spiritually blind (II Cor. 4:4) or spiritually deaf.
   B. Hope. "To him that overcometh will I give to eat of the tree of life, which is in the midst of the paradise of God." This speaks of heaven. Jesus promised us heaven (John 14:1-3). More is said of heaven in Revelation 20 and 21.

A church will be spiritual if the members are spiritual. It will be worldly if the members are worldly. No church can be stronger than its members. Peter gives a strict warning to the church members in I Peter 4:17, 18. All Christians would do well to examine their faith in God, as well as their dedication, lest they lose their first love as the Ephesians did.

4

THE SMYRMA CHURCH
Revelation 2:8-11

God constantly looks for those who are willing to stand for Him, serve Him, and suffer for Him. It is easy to accept the Lord, but is very difficult to follow Him fully. Many will accept Christ as Savior, but not as Lord and Master. When He is Lord and Master, He will have control over our lives. The people of Smyrna had made the Savior their Lord and Master.

I. THE CHURCH—v. 8
  A. The church—v. 8. Smyrna was about fifty miles northwest of Ephesus. This church was known for its endurance in serving the Lord.
  B. The character. This church was known for its suffering in the midst of suffering for the Lord. One cannot be a true child of God without suffering (II Tim. 3:12). Many serve the Lord when all is well, but when suffering and persecution come, they leave Him. This is the way it was for many who followed Jesus during His life on earth (John 6:66-68).

II. THE COMPLIMENT—v. 9
  A. Problem. "I know thy works and tribulation." God not only knows the suffering we bear for Him; He keeps a record.
  B. Poverty. "And poverty." We may be poor in the goods of this world, yet rich in heavenly things.

C. People. "And I know the blasphemy of them which say they are Jews, and are not, but are the synagogue of Satan."

It is not easy to stand for right when many oppose you. However, when you do stand for the truth, you do not stand alone—Jesus stands with you.

III. THE CONTROL—v. 10
  A. Fearless. "Fear none of those things which thou shalt suffer." God gives no promises of escaping suffering. (Note the words of Jesus in John 15:18, 19.)
  B. Faith. "Behold, the devil shall cast some of you into prison, that ye may be tried; and ye shall have tribulation ten days." We may have sufferings, but the Lord will care for us. He may not remove the trouble, but He will be with us in it.
  C. Faithfulness. "Be thou faithful unto death, and I will give thee a crown of life." Faithfulness is not only requested; it is required. (cf. Matt. 24:13).

IV. THE COMPENSATION—v. 11
  A. Listening. "Let him hear what the Spirit saith unto the churches." In simple words—"pay attention." We must not only hear, but obey what we hear.
  B. Life. "He that overcometh shall not be hurt of the second death." (Note the importance of living an overcoming Christian life, v. 7.) God's work is strengthened through overcoming Christians. Without such people, God's work is weakened.

Suffering for the Lord is a ministry. Though it is sometimes hard to accept, we know that God has a plan and purpose in all things (Rom. 8:28). A victorious Christian has an impact upon the non-Christian. A defeated Christian leaves another kind of impact upon the world: No one can have a successful Christian life. Be willing to suffer with Christ (cf. Mark 8:38).

5

THE PERGAMOS CHURCH
Revelation 2:12-17

The Pergamos church was known for its toleration of sin. One cannot tolerate sin in his life without it affecting his spiritual life. The same is true for churches. A compromising church will lose its influence and power. The person and church should hate sin, but love the sinner.

I.   **THE CHURCH**—vv. 12-13
    A. Place—v. 12. The Pergamos church was located fifty miles north of Smyrna.
    B. Persistence—v. 13. They were faithful to God in the midst of satanic power. Their faithfulness was revealed by the fact that they stayed true to God even after the slaying of Antipas. These people knew the reality of I John 4:4.
    C. God knew the people.
        1. I know thy works.
        2. I know where thou dwellest.
        3. Thou holdest fast my name.
        4. Thou hast not denied my name.

II. **THE COMPLAINT**—vv. 14-15
    A. Sinful problem—v. 14. "And yet I have a few things against you. You tolerate some among you who do as Balaam did when he taught Balak how to ruin the people of Israel by involving them in sexual sin and encouraging them to go to idol feasts" (LB).

B. Sinful practice—v. 15. The sins of Nicolaitanes were the sins of sexual impurity (adultery and fornication).

C. Sincere purity. Purity is a personal matter. See I Corinthians 6:19; II Corinthians 7:1; I John 2:15-17.

Christian liberty is not a license to live as we please. We must live according to the laws of God.

III. THE CHOICE—v. 16

A. Denouncement. The word *repent* has several meanings.
   1. To change
   2. Sorry enough to quit sinning
   3. Mourning for faults and failures (cf. Luke 13:3)

B. Destruction. If they did not repent, God would come and destroy them.

IV. THE COMPENSATION—v. 17

A. Opening. "He that hath an ear, let him hear what the Spirit saith unto the churches." Note the words, "They have ears, but they hear not" (Ps. 115:6).

B. Overcoming. "To him that overcometh will I give to eat of the hidden manna." This speaks of eternal life (John 3:16; 11:25-26). The white stone represents innocence; the black stone represents guilt.

The person who thinks lightly of sin, thinks lightly of God. All hidden sin will some day be revealed. If a person's sin is not revealed on earth, it will be revealed at the last great judgment day (Rev. 20:11-15). The church should not tolerate sin. Sin should be exposed, confessed, and removed. When this is done, God's power will come to the person, as well as to the church.

6

THE THYATIRA CHURCH
Revelation 2:18-29

One of Satan's favorite tools is compromise. The Thyatira church was full of compromisers. Compromise not only weakens the person and the church, it also opens the door to other sin which destroys God's work. It leads to indifference, lack of dedication, and finally, separation from God.

I. **THE CHURCH**—vv. 18-19
   A. Place. Thyatira was located between Pergamos and Sardis. The Thyatira church is sometimes called the church of worldly compromise.
   B. Personality. "This is a message from the Son of God, whose eyes penetrate like flames of fire, whose feet are like glowing brass" (LB). Christ has penetrating power—He sees all, and knows all.
   C. Praise—v. 19. The church was commended for six things.
      1. Works
      2. Charity
      3. Service
      4. Faith (really faithfulness)
      5. Patience
      6. Increased works. God records all our good works (Mal 3:16).

II. **THE COMPLAINT**—vv. 20-23
   A. Sin—v. 20. Jezebel (different than in I Kings 18-19) encouraged the people to commit sexual sins.
   B. Stubborn—v. 21. "I gave her time to change her mind and attitude but she refused" (LB).

C. Suffering—vv. 22-23. "Pay attention now to what I am saying: I will lay her upon a sickbed of intense affliction, along with all her immoral followers, unless they turn again to me, repenting of their sin with her, and I will strike her children dead. And all the churches shall know that I am he who searches deep within men's hearts, and minds; I will give to each of you whatever you deserve" (LB).

III. THE CONTROL—vv. 24-28
   A. False teaching—vv. 24-25. Jezebel was impressing upon the people that she was teaching "deeper truths" when she was really leading the people into deeper sin.
   B. Faithful in testing—vv. 26-27. Overcomers will be rewarded. Note that they will be given power over the nations (they will share in the millennial reign of Christ). Christ will give them the morning star (see Revelation 22:16).

Overcoming is the result of faithfulness. Overcoming is necessary for one to see God.

IV. THE CONSECRATION—v. 29
   Two-fold consecration is shown here:
   A. Hearing God's Word. We must hear God's Word with an open mind (cf. Rom. 10:17).
   B. Heeding God's Word. Hearing the Word is not enough; we must obey His Word (James 1:22).

Compromise is the first step downward for Christians. Compromise leads men away from God and allows Satan to have control in their lives. On the other hand, Satan fears consecrated Christians who live overcoming lives. Consecration leaves no room for indifference or compromise in the lives of believers.

7

THE SARDIS CHURCH
Revelation 3:1-6

Man often substitutes a religious life for a righteous life. There is a vast difference! Being religious is of man; being righteous is of God. Both man and churches fail to live righteous lives, so they live religious lives. God doesn't judge man by his outward appearance (religious actions), but by the heart (righteous life). When man's heart is righteous, then all phases of man's life will be righteous.

I. **THE CHURCH**—v. 1
   A. Place. Sardis was forty miles east of Smyrna, the ancient capital of Lydia.
   B. Person. God controls the seven Spirits of God and the seven stars.
   C. Problem. The church was active, but now is spiritually dead.

II. **THE CONCERN**—vv. 2-3
   A. Strengthen—v. 2. God instructed the people to strengthen what they had left. God is not interested in what they had in the past. He also wants us to use our resources to be up-to-date in living for Him and serving Him.
   B. Sober—v. 3. Christ will return as a thief and they who are asleep spiritually will miss Him.

   1. Sober—I Thessalonians 5:6. Be sober and alert.

   2. Solemn—Revelation 3:11. Let no man take thy crown.

   3. Serious—Revelation 16:15; Luke 12:37

Indifference should have no place in the life of a Christian. He should be serious about serving God at all times, knowing the coming of Christ is near.

III. THE CLEANLINESS—v. 4
To live a clean and holy life as those at Sardis did, requires two things.
  A. Cleansing. This cleansing begins with salvation (II Cor. 5:17). This cleansing must be maintained. Just as one takes a bath, one must have a spiritual bath. As we live in the light of God's Word, we will be cleansed by His blood (I John 1:7).
  B. Consecration. To live a holy life requires consecration. We must be fully surrendered unto the Lord. He must have first place in our lives (Matt. 6:33; see also Psalm 119:9, 11).

IV. THE COMPENSATION—vv. 5-6
  A. Overcoming—v. 5. Three promises are given to overcomers.
    1. They will be clothed in white raiment (Christ's righteousness).
    2. He will not blot their names from the book of life (salvation).
    3. He will confess them before God and the angels (heaven).
  B. Open—v. 6. Two-fold message:
    1. Listen to the Word of God.
    2. Learn from the Word of God.

God changes men at the time of conversion, however, there are choices for men to make after salvation. Paul said men must work out their own salvation (Phil. 2:12). As men choose the right ways, they will live righteous lives that are pleasing unto the Lord.

8

THE PHILADELPHIA CHURCH
Revelation 3:7-13

The Philadelphia church was not censored by the Lord; rather it was commended. Although some people disobey and reject the Lord, many others stand for righteousness and high principles. Love causes men to obey God and to follow His teachings.

I. **THE CHURCH**—v. 7
   A. Place. Philadelphia was thirty miles southeast of Sardis. It was known as the church of "brotherly love."
   B. Power. Power in speaking of the Lord:
      1. Purity. "He that is holy"
      2. Person. "He that is true."
      3. Power. "He that openeth, and no man shutteth; and shutteth, and no man openeth."

II. **THE CHARACTER**—vv. 8-9
   A. Personality—v. 8
      1. Observance. "I know thy works."
      2. Opening. "I have set before thee an open door, and no man can shut it."
      3. Obedience. "For thou hast a little strength, and hast kept my word and hast not denied my name."
   B. Power—v. 9. "Note this: 'I will force those supporting the causes of Satan while claiming to be mine (but they aren't—they are lying) to fall at your feet and acknowledge that you are the ones I love' " (LB).

III. **THE COMPENSATION**—v. 10
   A. Patience. They were patient despite persecution and problems. Patience is one of the most needed virtues today.

B. Promise. He will keep us in the hour of temptation. Some feel that this means that He will
keep us from going through the tribulation.

God is with man in temptation (I Cor. 10:13). He
permits no temptation without giving the power to
overcome it.

IV. THE CONTROL—vv. 11-13
A. Rapture—v. 11. We must hold to what we
have, so that Satan does not take our crown.
The Christian life is a battle (Eph. 6:12-18).
God gives us the tools to use in this battle.
B. Reward—v. 12. Our names will be written in
heaven. Note what happens to those whose
names were not written in God's Book (Rev.
20:11-15).
C. Respect—v. 13. Listen and heed what the Spirit says. Do more than hear—listen. Many hear,
but few ever listen or practice what they hear.

Many hear the teachings of God, but how many really
obey them? When one fully obeys, God's Word sinks
into the depths of his heart, changing him and making
him the person that God wants him to be. To be everything God wants you to be, you must do this concerning
God's Word: hear it, obey it, hide it, live it, share it,
study it, and know it. As we hide God's Word in our
heart, we will not sin against Him (Ps. 119:11). God's
Word will convict us of our sin (Heb. 4:12), cleanse us
from sin (Ps. 119:9), and increase our faith (Rom.
10:17).

9

THE LAODICEAN CHURCH
Revelation 3:14-22

Backsliding begins with indifference because indifference destroys dedication. The attitude of "do just

enough to get by" has hurt God's work more than one may realize. The people in the Laodicean church were living indifferent Christian lives.

I. **THE CHURCH**—vv. 14-15
   A. Place. Laodicea was a few miles west of Colosse.
   B. Person—v. 14. "This message is from the one who stands firm, the faithful and true Witness (of all that is or was or evermore shall be), the primeval source of God's creation" (LB).
   C. Problem—v. 15. God knew their works. The people were neither hot nor cold . . . they were lukewarm. Jesus said if we are not for Him, we are against Him (Matt. 12:30).

II. **THE COMPLAINTS**—vv. 16-17
   A. Sickness—v. 16. The Laodiceans' way of life made God sick and He would spew the Laodiceans out of His mouth.
   B. Satisfaction—v. 17. The Laodiceans found satisfaction in a way which did not, nor will ever please God. They said:
      1. I am rich. They were rich with earthly things.
      2. I am increased with goods. They had no need for material things.
      3. I have need of nothing. They had no need for earthly things.

When one feels he has all that he needs, he is in great danger. Jesus said, "Without me, ye can do nothing" (John 15:5).

III. **THE COUNSEL**—vv. 18-19
   A. Counsel—v. 18. Note the four-fold request of the Lord to the people at Laodicea:
      1. Buy of me gold tried in the fire. This means faith (I Peter 1:7).

29

2. Buy of me white raiment. This means righteousness.
3. Anoint thy eyes with eyesalve. This means enlightenment (Ps. 19:8).
4. Be zealous and repent. This means sorrow. (See Luke 13:3.)

B. Chastening—v. 19. "I continually discipline and punish everyone I love; so I must punish you, unless you turn from your indifference and become enthusiastic about the things of God" (LB).

IV. THE CHRIST—v. 20
A. Person. "Behold I [Jesus]."
B. Place. "Stand at the door [heart's door] and knock."
C. Pleasure. "If any man hear my voice, and opens the door, I will come in to him, and will sup with him, and he with me."

V. THE COMPENSATION—vv. 21-22
A. Overcoming—v. 21. Overcomers will be with the Lord in heaven (John 14:1-3).
B. Open—v. 22. Keep open to the Spirit. Allow Him to speak to you.

Christ has no need for indifferent or slipshod workers. The only cure for indifference is dedication. The Laodicean church members once had this dedication, but became indifferent. If one loses God's touch upon his life by being indifferent, he has a negative impact upon others—he leads them astray.

10

THE OPEN DOOR
Revelation 4:1-11

God does reveal certain things to His people. Jesus gave the promise of heaven in John 14:1-3. Later Paul spoke of the indescribable beauty of heaven (I Cor. 2:9). Now God opens the door to heaven and explains to John the beauty of heaven. Heaven is a real place. It is for all those who meet God's requirements for salvation.

I. **THE PLACE**—vv. 1-3
   A. Person—v. 1. God showed John the glories of the future that are for God's people.
   B. Place—v. 2. Vision of heaven. John saw the throne of God.
   C. Personality—v. 3. "Great bursts of light flashed forth from him as from a glittering diamond, or from a shining ruby, and a rainbow glowing like an emerald encircles his throne" (LB).

II. **THE PEOPLE**—vv. 4-5
   A. People—v. 4. This is no doubt the rapture of the church. The twenty-four elders perhaps mean the twelve tribes of Israel, representing the Old Testament and the twelve disciples, representing the New Testament (cf. Rev. 21:12-14).
   B. Picture—vv. 5-6
      1. Throne of judgment. The lightning and thunder was seen as in Exodus 20:18 (cf. Heb. 12:18-21).
      2. The lamps represent the Holy Spirit (Isa. 11:2).
      3. The sea of glass was transparent, meaning it had no blemish.

III. **THE PRAISE**—vv. 7-8
   A. Appearance—v. 7. The first beast was like a lion, the second beast was like a calf, the third beast had a man's face, and the fourth beast was like an eagle.

B. Attitude—v. 8. The seraphim's job was to praise God at all times (cf. Isa. 6:1-8). They praised the One "which was, and is, and is to come."

IV. **THE PLEASURE**—vv. 9-11

A. Persons—vv. 9-10a. "And when the Living Beings gave glory and honor and thanks to the one sitting on the throne, who lives forever and ever, the twenty-four Elders fell down before him and worshiped him, the Eternal Living One" (LB).

B. Praise—v. 10. The elders bowed down and cast their crowns before Him in their praise to Him.

C. Pleasure—v. 11. "Thou art worthy, O Lord, to receive glory and honour and power." God made man to praise Him. "For thou hast created all things, and for thy pleasure they are and were created."

God longs to have men's worship. If men don't know how to worship the Lord here, they will feel out of place in heaven. The Bible has much to say about praise and thanks. Prayer is stressed in today's churches, but praise is given little emphasis. One of the best ways to pray is to praise. Praise opens a person to God and heavenly things.

11

THE CLOSED BOOK
Revelation 5:1-14

God has hidden many things from man. "For my thoughts are not your thoughts, neither are your ways my ways, saith the Lord. For as the heavens are higher than the earth, so are my ways higher than your ways,

and my thoughts than your thoughts" (Isa. 55:8, 9).
God has a plan and purpose in all things (Rom. 8:28).
He is not early nor late in revealing His will.

I. **THE PROBLEM**—vv. 1-4
A. The sealed book—v. 1. The book was sealed with seven seals. No one knew the contents of this book except God.
B. The sacred book—vv. 2-3
1. Question—v. 2. Who is worthy to open the book? Who will loosen its seals?
2. Answer—v. 3. No one on earth, or heaven (except Christ) was worthy to open this book.
C. The sorrow because of the book—v. 4. "Then I wept with disappointment because no one anywhere was worthy; no one could tell us what it said" (LB).

II. **THE PERSON**—vv. 5-7
A. Comfort—v. 5. The Lion of the tribe of Judah, the Root of David, was able to open the book. Only Jesus, the all powerful one could open it.
B. Christ—v. 6. John called Jesus the Lamb of God (John 1:29).
C. Control—v. 7. The omnipotent and eternal Christ took the book from God.

III. **THE PRACTICE**—vv. 8-10
A. Worship—v. 8. The elders bowed down and worshiped Christ. Worship is a practice all Christians should do daily.
B. Worthy—vv. 9-10. The elders sang a new song. In ourselves we are not worthy to see God, but through His death, Christ made us worthy. God made us His sons and daughters. Because we belong to Him, we shall reign with Him in all His glory.

IV. THE PRAISE—vv. 11-14

A. People—v. 11. Countless numbers of angels praised God. The Living Bible says there were "millions."

B. Praise—v. 12. Worthy is the Lamb that was slain to receive:
   1. Power
   2. Riches
   3. Wisdom
   4. Strength
   5. Honor
   6. Glory
   7. Blessing

C. Practice—vv. 13-14. All creatures worshiped the Lamb. Praise and worship are not optional —they are required.

All Christians should read Psalm 100 often and practice the words of the psalmist in their daily lives. At times we do not understand God's Word or will for our lives. But during these times, we must trust Him for He knows what is best for us.

12

OPENING THE SIX SEALS
Revelation 6:1-17

To understand Revelation, one must study the Book of Daniel. Note the prayers of Daniel in Daniel 9:3, 17, 19. Daniel 9:24 speaks of sealing the vision. Now the vision, or seals are opened. Although there are seven seals, the seventh is different than the other six.

I. THE FIRST SEAL—vv. 1-2

A. Power—v. 1. John witnessed the Lamb (Jesus) opening the first seal. One of the four beasts said in a loud voice, "Come and see."

B. Picture—v. 2. The rider on the white horse is the Antichrist who goes forth to conquer. He decieves people into thinking that he is Christ by riding a white horse. This is the start of the terrible events of the tribulation.

II. **THE SECOND SEAL**—vv. 3-4
   A. Antichrist—v. 3. The second beast said, "Come and see."
   B. Awfulness—v. 4. The red horse represented war. Satan has always destroyed life. Now he works through the Antichrist to destroy mankind. (Note the contrast between Christ and Satan in John 10:9, 10.)

III. **THE THIRD SEAL**—vv. 5-6
   A. Power—v. 5. The black horse stood for famine. The Antichrist will take control on the earth, since all Christians and the Holy Spirit will be with Christ after the rapture.
   B. Problem—v. 6. Inflation will know no bounds. The Living Bible says a loaf of bread will cost twenty dollars.

IV. **THE FOURTH SEAL**—vv. 7-8
   As this seal is opened Satan uses two things he has always used against God's people.
   A. Death. The pale horse is death. He destroys love, liberty, and life.
   B. Destruction. Since the time God created man, Satan has been busy destroying the things of God and God's people.

V. **THE FIFTH SEAL**—vv. 9-11
   A. Preaching—v. 9. John saw the souls under the altar of those who preached the gospel during the tribulation and those who refused the mark of the beast and were saved.

B. Plea—v. 10. They asked God how long they must suffer for Him.
C. Patience—v. 11. They were encouraged to be patient, since many others would be martyred for the sake of the gospel.

VI. **THE SIXTH SEAL**—vv. 12-17
   A. Power—vv. 12-14. An earthquake then shakes the world, but does not destroy it. It is not yet God's time for this.
   B. People—vv. 15-17. Men are fearful. They try to escape God's judgment. But who is able to survive?

Many believe we shall escape the tribulation and all its suffering. However, suppose we didn't escape it. Would you have enough of God's power and enough dedication to stand the awful suffering that will come during this time? It may be easy to die for Christ, but to suffer would require greater dedication.

13
THE TRIBULATION CHRISTIANS
Revelation 7:1-17

Though the Holy Spirit will be removed with the saints at the time of the rapture, others will be saved during the tribulation. However, these must be willing to give their lives, since they will not accept the mark of the beast. These people will be those who hear the gospel before the rapture, yet reject it. Later they will see their folly and accept Christ.

I. **THE PROTECTION**—vv. 1-8
   A. Peace—v. 1. "Then I saw four angels standing at the four corners of the earth, holding back the four winds from blowing, so that not a leaf

rustled in the trees, and the ocean became as smooth as glass" (LB).

B. Protection—vv. 2-3. The angel holds back the punishment upon those who were saved during the tribulation and had God's seal upon their foreheads.

C. People—vv. 4-8. From the tribes of Israel 144,000 were saved—12,000 from each of the twelve tribes. Note the use of the number *twelve* in Revelation (gates, tribes, foundations, apostles, thousand furlongs).

II. THE PEOPLE—vv. 9-12

A. People—v. 9. An innumerable amount of people from all nations surrounded the throne. They were clothed in white which represented the righteousness of Christ. The palms in their hands stood for victory. This group is different than the 144,000.

B. Praise—v. 10. They praised God for their salvation which was provided by the Lamb.

C. Pleasure—v. 11. They took pleasure in thanking and praising God. Showing appreciation for the price of our salvation should be the practice of all Christians.

D. Power—v. 12. " 'Amen!' they said. 'Blessing, and glory, and wisdom, and thanksgiving, and honor, and power, and might, be to our God forever and forever. Amen!' " (LB).

III. THE PEACE—13-17

A. The people—vv. 13-14

1. Question—v. 13. Who are these in the white robes? Where did they come from?

2. Answer—v. 14. They came out of the tribulation. They could be called "the tribulation saints." Their robes were washed in the

blood of the Lamb. (See Romans 10:13; I John 1:7.)

B. The practice—v. 15. These people were before God daily, serving Him. See the importance of worshiping God in His house (Ps. 122:1; Heb. 10:25).

C. The protection—v. 16. God always protects His children.

D. The peace—v. 17. God will help them, comfort them, and will even wipe the tears from their eyes.

One should not say, "I'll wait until the tribulation to accept Christ." No one knows if he will live that long. On the other hand, if a person cannot accept Christ with the saints present and with the Holy Spirit convicting, how will he come to Christ during this difficult time? Christ's coming may be near or it could be years from now. In the meantime, death may come, giving a person no second chance for salvation.

14

FIRST FOUR TRUMPETS
Revelation 8:1-13

The opening of the seventh seal is the end of the first three and one-half years of the tribulation, and the beginning of the second three and one-half years and the sounding of the trumpets. The first half of the tribulation is mild in comparison to the second half. The second half of the tribulation will bring more trouble, heartache, and sorrow.

I. **SILENCE BEFORE THE TRUMPETS**—v. 1

    A. Seal. The seventh seal is now opened. The opening of this seal is the beginning of the suf-

fering of man during the time of the tribulation.
  B. Silence. There is silence for one-half hour. No reason is given for this silence.

II. **SYMBOLS OF THE TRUMPETS**—vv. 2-6
  Keep in mind that there are many symbols used in the Book of Revelation to explain a truth.
  A. Preparation—v. 2. The seven angels stand before God, and are given seven trumpets.
  B. Prayers—vv. 3-4. Incense and the prayers of God's people are presented before the throne of God.
  C. Punishments—v. 5. The awful punishments are about to start. Men will not be able to hold these back.
  D. Plan—v. 6. The angels prepare to sound the trumpets. Angels always do God's bidding, without asking questions or making excuses.

III. **SOUNDING OF TRUMPETS**—vv. 7-13
  A. First trumpet—v. 7. The sound of the first trumpet announced God's curse upon nature.
    1. Hail and fire mingled with blood was cast upon the earth.
    2. One-third of the trees and all green grass was burned up.
  B. Second trumpet—vv. 8-9
    1. A great mountain burning with fire was cast into the sea.
    2. One-third of the sea became blood.
    3. One-third of the sea creatures and other living things in the sea died.
    4. One-third of the ships were destroyed.
  C. Third trumpet—vv. 10-11. A falling star or meteor fell on one-third of the rivers and on fountains of water causing them to become

wormwood. Many men died from drinking the water.
D. Fourth trumpet—v. 12. One-third of the sun, moon, and stars was smitten and darkened. Daylight was dimmed and nighttime darkness was deepened.
E. Last three trumpets—v. 13. The last three trumpet judgments would be even worse than the first four.

Satan has created suffering, heartache, and problems for men since creation. Because God will not use His restraining power during the tribulation, there will be almost no limit to the suffering men will face because of Satan's power. All men who are ready to meet Christ at the rapture will escape this tribulation.

15
FIVE MONTHS OF SUFFERING
Revelation 9:1-21

When Satan is in control he shows no mercy. As the tribulation continues, we not only see Satan's power increasing; we see men suffering more and more.

I. THE SCENE—vv. 1-2
   A. Star—v. 1. Some people feel that this fallen star may be a fallen angel, possibly Satan (Isa. 14:12-15). God referred to angels as stars (Job 38:7).
   B. Suffering—v. 2. The star was given the keys to the bottomless pit (abyss). Some feel that this is the abode of demons. Later Satan will be cast into the pit to suffer.

II. THE SUPERNATURAL—vv. 3-11
   A. Power—vv. 3-5. Locusts with supernatural power will come forth to hurt men that do not

have the seal of God in their foreheads. They will sting men for five months.

B. Problem—v. 6. Men will seek death, but will not find it. They will be kept alive to face this suffering.

C. Practice—vv. 7-11. Here we see the description of the locusts. They will be led by a king who is Satan or the Antichrist.

III. **THE SORROW**—vv. 12-17

A. Announcement—v. 12. There are two woes of more suffering and sorrow to come.

B. Angels—vv. 13-14. The sixth trumpet is about to sound. The four angels that were bound in the Euphrates River (near Eden, Gen. 2:14) could have been those who sinned with Lucifer. God didn't spare the angels who sinned (II Peter 2:4).

C. Awfulness—vv. 15-16. These four angels are now loosed. They were saved for this time to kill one-third of all mankind. They had an army of 200 million warriors.

D. Allegory—vv. 17-19. "I saw their horses spread out before me in my vision; their riders wore fiery-red breastplates, though some were sky-blue and others yellow. The horses' heads looked much like lions', and smoke and fire and flaming sulphur billowed from their mouths, killing one-third of all mankind. Their power of death was not only in their mouths, but in their tails as well, for their tails were similar to serpents' heads that struck and bit with fatal wounds" (LB).

IV. **THE STUBBORNESS**—vv. 20-21

A. Stubborn. The men not killed by the plagues refused to repent of their sins. They hardened their hearts to the things of God.

B. Sins. These people would not repent of their various sins.
   1. Demon worship
   2. Idolatry
   3. Murder
   4. Sorcery
   5. Fornication
   6. Thefts

It is unusual that men would rather follow Satan who tortures them than God who loves them.

16

THE MIGHTY ANGEL
Revelation 10:1-11

During the period of the tribulation, Satan will remain in control. Later, his power will come to an end. Here we see an angel (Jesus Christ) explaining the truths of the future to John. God has not left us in the dark; He wants us to know the events of the future.

I. **THE POWER OF THE ANGEL**—vv. 1-4
   A. Personality—vv. 1-2. The angel is Jesus. Note His appearance:
      1. Clothed in a cloud (cf. Exod. 13:21; 34:5; Acts 1:9).
      2. Rainbow upon His hand (see Genesis 9:13; Revelation 4:3).
      3. Face as the sun (see Malachi 4:2, Matthew 17:2, Acts 26:13).
      4. Feet as pillars of fire (see Revelation 1:15). Brass is a symbol of judgment and fire is a symbol of wrath.
      5. A little book open in His hand. Some feel that it is the seven-sealed book of Revela-

tion 5; others feel it is the book mentioned in Daniel 12:9.

6. His right foot on the sea and left foot on the earth. He takes possession of the earth.

B. Power—vv. 3-4
1. Crying with a loud voice—v. 3. (See Joel 3:14-16.)
2. Seven thunders—v. 4. This could be God's response. God did not permit John to record what the voices said.

III. THE PROMISE BY THE ANGEL—vv. 5-7
A. Power—v. 5. Christ lifted His hand toward heaven, showing His authority and power.
B. Prayer—v. 6 Earlier the martyrs asked the Lord how long they would have to suffer. There would be no delay now.
C. Plan—v. 7. "But that when the seventh angel blew his trumpet, then God's veiled plan—mysterious through the ages ever since it was announced by his servants the prophets—would be fulfilled" (LB).

IV. THE PLAN SHOWN BY THE ANGEL—vv. 8-11
A. Speaking—v. 8. The voice from heaven said to John, "Take the little book." This is the book spoken of in Revelation 5.
B. Sharing—v. 9. (Cf. Ezek. 2:9, 10; 3:1-4, 14.) Use Scripture to interpret Scripture.
C. Sweet—v. 10. The book was sweet in John's mouth, but bitter in his belly. There was some pleasing and unpleasing intelligence in the book. God's people would now be safe, but John could still remember their persecution and sorrow.
D. Showing—v. 11. John was instructed to prophesy before the people to show them their

wrong and to warn them of God's impending judgment.

God's Word not only shows men their sin; it gives a cure for that sin. It not only tells of future tribulation; it shows God's mercy. Men must either accept or reject God's plan for salvation. If men face the tribulation, it is because they choose to.

17

THE TWO WITNESSES
Revelation 11:1-19

The sufferings of the tribulation continue. In this chapter, we see the two witnesses coming to earth to speak. Despite their message, they are not accepted. Sin despises righteousness and godly warnings and teachings. Although men know the rapture will have already taken place, they will not change their attitudes toward God.

I. **THE PROPHECY**—vv. 1-3
    A. Temple—v. 1. John was given a reed (twelve and one-half feet long) to measure the temple.
    B. Trample—v. 2. He was told not to measure the court. It was to be trampled for three and one-half years (forty-two months). This is spoken of in Daniel 12:7.
    C. Testimony—v. 3. The two witnesses will minister for three and one-half years. These witnesses may be Enoch and Elijah, since neither died.

II. **THE PICTURE**—vv. 4-6
    A. Picture—v. 4. The angel called the witnesses olive trees (cf. Zech. 4). The Holy Spirit rests upon the witnesses.
    B. Protection—v. 5. Anyone who tries to destroy these witnesses will be destroyed by fire.

C. Power—v. 6. The witnesses will be able to perform miracles as Moses did (Exod. 7:20; see Elijah in I Kings 17:1; James 5:17).

III. THE PREACHING—vv. 7-10
   A. Death—v. 7. After three and one-half years of preaching, the beast (same as in Revelation 13:1; 17:8) kills the witnesses.
   B. Deserted—vv. 8-9. People will fear touching the witnesses. The witnesses will lie in the street for three and one-half days. Sodom and Egypt mean Jerusalem.
   C. Delight—v. 10. People will rejoice over the death of these two witnesses.

IV. THE POWER—vv. 11-14
   A. Translation—vv. 11-12. The two witnesses will be translated into heaven. Though they were dead for three and one-half days, the Spirit will enter their bodies and they will be resurrected.
   B. Trouble—vv. 13-14. An earthquake will cause the deaths of 7,000 people. Some people will fear God and give Him glory at this time. The second woe is past; the third woe will soon start.

V. THE PLAN—vv. 15-19
   A. Plan—v. 15. The seventh trumpet sounds. Christ shall reign over His kingdom now. Some feel this period will cover three and one-half years.
   B. Praise—vv. 16-17. The twenty-four elders fell on their faces and worshiped God. Again they called Him the one "which art, and wast, and art to come."
   C. People—v. 19. The Antichrist will rise against Christ.
   D. Picture—v. 19. The ark of the covenant was seen in the temple in heaven.

18

THE WAR IN HEAVEN
Revelation 12:1-17

I. **SATAN.** Never underestimate him.
   A. His power. He can perform supernatural acts.
   B. His plan. His plan has been and will always be to destroy.
   C. His personality. He deceives by changing his personality.
   D. His persistence. He never quits. He seeks to destroy all that is of God.

II. **THE SYMBOL**—vv. 1-6
   A. Picture—vv. 1-2. The woman represents Israel as a nation. She has a crown with twelve stars which represent the twelve tribes of Israel. The child is Christ (Ps. 2:9; Isa. 66:7; Rev. 19:15).
   B. Person—v. 3. The red dragon symbolizes Satan. The seven heads are a symbol of the seven empires that proceed the kingdom of Christ. The ten horns are a symbol of earthly power.
   C. Problem—vv. 4-6
      1. Plan—v. 4. Satan planned to destroy Christ as soon as He was born. We have seen this conflict since Genesis 3:15.
      2. Protection—v. 5. Christ ascended from earth to God's throne.
      3. Projection—v. 6. This is an anticipation of what is described in vv. 13-15.

III. **THE SACREDNESS**—vv. 7-12
   Evil cannot triumph over good without the permission of God.
   A. Scene—v. 7. There was war in heaven. Michael and his angels fought against Satan and his angels. Michael is mentioned in Daniel 10:13.

B. Satan—vv. 8-9. Christ has power and control over the dragon. The dragon is called Devil, Satan, and Deceiver.
C. Savior—vv. 10-11
 1. Salvation—v. 10. When Satan was cast out, salvation, strength, the kingdom of God, and the power of Christ came.
 2. Surrender—v. 11. God's people overcame Satan by the blood of Christ, and the word of their testimony. Their lives were secondary compared to their love for Christ.
D. Sorrow—v. 12. Satan will not give up. He will increase his power.

IV. **THE SUPERNATURAL**—vv. 13-17
Satan uses his supernatural power.
A. Persecution—v. 13. The dragon persecuted the woman.
B. Protection—v. 14. The woman flees for protection from the dragon.
C. Power—v. 15. Note the power of the dragon (cf. Ps. 18:4).
D. Providence—v. 16. Earth opens and swallows the water which the dragon uses to destroy the woman (see Num. 16:32).

Satan is powerful, but God's power is greater. God is on our side no matter who is against us (Rom. 8:31). If God lives within us, we are greater than he (Satan) who is in the world. With God's power, we can overcome all sin and be what God wants us to be.

19

THE TWO BEASTS
Revelation 13:1-18

This chapter is difficult to interpret. This chapter tells of the two beasts who will take control during this portion of the tribulation. They will have great power given to them by Satan. Men cannot cope with the powers of Satan without the help of God.

I. **THE CHARACTER OF THE FIRST BEAST—** vv. 1-4

   A. Appearance—v. 1. This beast came from the sea. The sea represents the confused Gentile nations. This beast bears some relationship to Daniel's beast. This is the same beast as mentioned in Revelation 17. The ten horns are explained in Daniel 7:24; Revelation 17:12.
   B. Allegory—v. 2. For reference see Daniel 7:4-8, 23-24; 8:20; 11:40-45. Daniel had a vision of four beasts. They looked like a lion, a bear, and a leopard, and one beast was undescribed.
   C. Affection—vv. 3-4. Note the satanic power the dragon gave to the beast to perform miracles and to work wonders. People will worship him. No human power seems to compare with his power.

II. **THE CONTROL OF THE BEAST—vv. 5-10**

   A. Cursing—vv. 5-6. For forty-two months the beast curses the name of the Lord and the Lord's people.
   B. Control—vv. 7-8. The beast will have power to make war against God's people. He will have power over all people, who do not have their names in God's Book.
   C. Concern—v. 9. If you hear God's voice, obey Him.
   D. Captivity—v. 10. This verse should be interpreted with Jeremiah 15:2; 43:11.

III. **THE CHARACTER OF THE SECOND BEAST**
—vv. 11-18
   A. Appearance—v. 11. This beast comes out of
   the earth. He looks like a lamb, but acts like a
   dragon (cf. Matt. 7:15).
   B. Actions—vv. 12-15. Note his actions:
      1. Supernatural—vv. 12-13
         a. Healing—v. 12
         b. Great wonders. Fire comes down from
         heaven—v. 13.
         c. Miracles—v. 14
         d. Gives life—v. 15
      2. Slavery—vv. 16-17. Without his mark the
      people cannot buy or sell, and will therefore
      die (possible starvation).
      3. Sign—v. 18. His number will be 666.

For every real thing, Satan has a counterfeit. He uses
counterfeits to destroy God's work.

20

THE SIX ANGELS
Revelation 14:1-20

This chapter deals with the six angels and their mes-
sages. It deals also with the sealed 144,000. It tells how
they were taken to be with the Lord and how they
praise the Lord.

I. **THE SAVIOR APPEARS**—vv. 1-5
   A. Appearance—v. 1. The Lamb appeared with
   the 144,000 who all had the Father's name (or
   seal) upon their foreheads. This is the same
   group that is spoken of in Revelation 7:1-8.
   B. Actions—vv. 2-5
      1. Praise—vv. 2-5. They played harps and sang
      praises unto the Lord. They sang a new

song—a song of redemption—which no one else could learn.

2. Perfection—v. 5. They were made perfect in the Lord. Only the Lord can purify men to make them holy in the sight of God.

II. **THE SIX ANGELS**—vv. 6-20
   A. First angel—vv. 6-27
      1. The preacher—the angel
      2. The pulpit—in the midst of heaven
      3. The preaching—the everlasting gospel
      4. The people—every nation, kindred, and people on earth
   B. Second angel—v. 8. The downfall of Babylon is spoken of in Revelation 17.
   C. Third angel—vv. 9-11. There is no hope for those who worship the beast or receive his mark. They will be tormented day and night in fire and brimstone.
      1. Saints—vv. 12-13. The Christians patiently kept the commandments of God and the faith of Jesus.
      2. Savior—v. 14. He has a crown (He is King) and a sickle (He will go forth to reap). (See Matthew 13:30, 39; 24:30, 31.)
   D. Fourth angel—vv. 15-16. Christ was sent forth to reap. This is what will happen at Armageddon. (See the following chapters of Revelation.)
   E. Fifth angel—v. 17. The fifth angel is concerned about gathering the grape clusters.
   F. Sixth angel—vv. 18-20
      1. The altar is mentioned also in 6:9; 8:3; and 16:7.
      2. The vine is a symbol of a religious system. (See Psalm 80:8-11; Isaiah 5:1-7.)

3. The winepress is a symbol of the wrath of God which is to come.

4. "Blood flowed out in a stream 200 miles long and as high as a horse's bridle" (v. 20b, LB).

It is important to be ready to meet the Lord when the rapture takes place. Thank God for making a way of escape from this terrible time.

21

SUFFERING AND SORROW
Revelation 15:1-8

Throughout the Bible we read of men who suffered for the cause of Christ. These men had the Holy Spirit to comfort them at their lowest times. Thus it is for today's Christians. But those who refuse to accept Christ's love today will have to face the much more terrible trials of the tribulation alone.

I. **THE SUFFERING**—vv. 1-4
   A. Plagues—v. 1. God's wrath continues. The seven angels bring this wrath. The word *seven* is used fifty-four times in Revelation.
   B. Picture—vv. 2-3
      1. Symbol—v. 2. John saw a sea of glass mingled with fire. This is probably the same sea as in Revelation 4:6. The fire may be a symbol of the sufferings that must soon come to pass (see I Peter 4:12-13). These sufferings continue until Revelation 19. Notice, the people on the sea had "gotten the victory over the beast." Their victory had cost them their lives.
      2. Song—v. 3. They sang a song of Moses (see Exod. 15:1-9; Deut. 32).

C. Personality—v. 4. Because God is holy, we should honor and respect Him. "All nations will worship Him" is a prophecy of the millennial reign of Christ.

II. **THE SORROW**—vv. 5-8
A. Purity—v. 5. The temple is opened. It was opened before in Revelation 11:19. The temple of the Old Testament was holy. This temple is not in the new Jerusalem, since there will be no temple there. This one is called the "tabernacle of the testimony." It may be called this because the Ten Commandments which were kept in the ark were later taken to the temple. Contrast the holiness of the Lord with the sinfulness of man.
B. Personality—v. 6. Seven angels appear.
   1. White linen—symbol of righteousness.
   2. Golden girdles—righteousness and faithfulness of God.
C. Power—v. 7. The angels are given seven vials which contain the wrath of God. Although God is patient and kind, there is a limit to His patience. If men reject God's love and kindness, His judgment must fall.
D. Problem—v. 8. The temple is filled with smoke from the glory of God. No man was able to enter the temple until after the seven plagues were fulfilled.

God has never promised to remove all of men's sufferings and sorrows. However, at times He does remove them. In other cases, He gives men strength to endure suffering. The age-old question, "Why do the righteous suffer?" can be answered by God alone. The child of God has the assurance that there is a purpose for his sufferings and that God is doing His will. Sinners have no help during their sufferings.

22

THE SEVEN VIALS
Revelation 16:1-21

Though God's wrath continues and suffering increases, it won't last long. Soon the Antichrist will be defeated and his control and reign will end. God permits the forces of evil to go only so far before He intercedes.

I. **THE VIALS**—v. 1
The angels are told to go and pour out the seven vials (the wrath of God) upon man during the tribulation.

II. **THE FIRST VIAL**—v. 2
A. A sore came upon all men who accepted the mark of the beast (666).
B. They accepted this mark so that they might live. Now they paid for it with terrible suffering.

III. **THE SECOND VIAL**—v. 3
A. The second vial turned the sea into blood.
B. All the creatures in the sea died. Because of man's sin and stubbornness, God's judgment even falls upon the creatures of the sea.

IV. **THE THIRD VIAL**—vv. 4-7
A. Change—v. 4. The rivers and fountains became blood. (Could this be the same as in Exodus 7:19-24?)
B. Christ—vv. 5-7. Since Christians and God's prophets had to shed their blood for what they believed, Christ gave their murderers blood to drink. God's judgments are true and just.

V. **THE FOURTH VIAL**—vv. 8-9
A. Suffering—v. 8. A vial was poured out upon the sun. It scorched men with fire.

B. Stubborn—v. 9. Still men would not repent. Instead they cursed God. Men's sufferings will only harden their hearts.

VI. THE FIFTH VIAL—vv. 10-11
A. Suffering—v. 10. The beast's kingdom became dark and men gnawed their tongues in pain.
B. Stubborn—v. 11. They cursed God and refused to repent.

VII. THE SIXTH VIAL—vv. 12-16
A. Sorrow—v. 12. The Euphrates River dried up so that the armies could march through.
B. Spirits—v. 13. Three unclean spirits came out of the mouth of the dragon, beast and false prophet.
C. Supernatural—v. 14. The spirits had great power.
D. Sober—v. 15. Be ready for His return at all times.
E. Suffering—v. 16. The battle of Armageddon is soon to happen.

VIII. THE SEVENTH VIAL—vv. 17-21
A. Completion—v. 17. The completion of the tribulation is near.
B. Confusion—vv. 18-21. Jerusalem was the headquarters of the beast. Babylon means heathen Rome. Hailstones weighing up to 100 pounds would fall.

The Christian has hope because his suffering will soon be over. The sinner has no such hope. He may suffer all his life, reject Christ, and be sent to hell, where he will suffer eternally. The Christian may suffer for years, but in eternity he will know no suffering.

23

THE GREAT HARLOT
Revelation 17:1-18

The religious, commercial, and political structure of Babylon will be destroyed. The religious system will perish through the power of the ten kings. Later Babylon's commerce will fall, for no one will buy her goods. The merchants of the earth shall weep and mourn over her. Babylon's political structure will be destroyed at Christ's appearing.

I. **HER POSITION**—vv. 1-3
   - A. Personality—v. 1. John was invited to come and see what would happen to the great whore. She represents a corrupt church.
   - B. Power—v. 2. The woman has seduced men and nations from serving God, and living for Him.
   - C. Position—v. 3. She fled to the wilderness, because of the coming judgment. The beast is the same as in Revelation 13:1. Scarlet is a symbol of the shed blood. The ten horns are explained in vv. 9-12.

II. **HER PERSONALITY**—vv. 4-6
   - A. Picture—v. 4. She may have worn purple to imitate Christ. (Some scholars say she was dressed in the colors of the papal church of Roman cardinals' garments. Others say she was dressed the same as other harlots of her time.) The golden cup is the same as mentioned in Jeremiah 51:7.
   - B. Person—v. 5. Her name, Babylon the Great, was given to her by her followers. She is sometimes referred to as the mother of harlots.
   - C. Problem—v. 6. She was drunk on the blood of the saints and of the ones who refused to worship the Antichrist.

III. HER POWER—vv. 7-14

A. Person—v. 7. Her power is given by the Antichrist. The seven heads and ten horns are explained later.

B. Prediction—v. 8. Here we see a prediction of the downfall of the Antichrist.

C. Prophecy—v. 9. This prophecy may be better understood by reading Daniel 12:10. The seven mountains (hills of Rome) are the headquarters of the woman.

D. People—vv. 10-11. Five kings have already fallen, one is reigning and one is yet to come. The eighth one is the Antichrist.

E. ·Power—vv. 12-14

1. Picture—v. 12. The ten horns, ten kings will come later to make war.

2. Power—v. 13. They will join one another for power in unity.

3. Prophecy—v. 14. This battle will be at Armageddon. Christians will be with Christ in this battle.

IV. HER PEOPLE—vv. 15-18

A. People—v. 15. This is a picture of the masses of people.

B. Problem—vv. 16-17. Her followers will desert her, not knowing they are fulfilling God's plan in doing so.

C. Picture—v. 18. The great harlot and Babylon are one.

24

THE FALL OF BABYLON
Revelation 18:1-24

See Jeremiah 50—51 for a better understanding of the following Scripture.

I. **SEPARATION**—vv. 1-3
    A. Person—v. 1. An angel with great power appears. This most likely is Jesus Christ.
    B. Personality—v. 2. "He gave a mighty shout, 'Babylon the Great is fallen, is fallen; she has become a den of demons, a haunt of devils and every kind of evil spirit' " (LB).
    C. Practice—v. 3. Babylon is a commercial center. The nations have become rich by accepting her and rejecting God.

II. **SORROW**—vv. 4-10
    A. Person—v. 4. Another voice from heaven asked the people to separate themselves from Babylon's sins.
    B. Punishment—vv. 5-8
        1. Remembrance—v. 5. God knew of Babylon's sins.
        2. Reward—v. 6. She would receive twice the punishment that she gave to others.
        3. Remorse—v. 7. She had lived in luxury, but now she would be forsaken and forgotten.
        4. Removed—v. 8. She is removed from her place and destroyed.
    C. People—vv. 9-10. Those who followed her will see her downfall. She was great, but was now brought down.

III. **SUFFERING**—vv. 11-20
    A. Desolation—vv. 11-16. No one will buy Babylon's goods, since she has fallen. They have lost faith in her.
    B. Destruction—vv. 17-19. It seems impossible that the great Babylon could be so swiftly demolished.
    C. Delight—v. 20. The saints could rejoice now that this sinful city was destroyed. God repaid Babylon for leading people astray.

A person who serves Satan may feel that he is a success in this life. But he must remember that his success will be short lived.

IV. **SUPERNATURAL**—vv. 21-24
   A. Denounced—v. 21. God's judgment was so great that Babylon would never be rebuilt (Jer. 51:59-64).
   B. Decree—vv. 22-23. No more business would be carried on in this sinful city.
   C. Death—v. 24. Babylon was responsible for the death and destruction of the prophets and saints.

25

COMPLETE VICTORY
Revelation 19:1-21

I. **THE CHOIR**—vv. 1-7
   A. People—v. 1. John heard "much people" praising God. These are the ones who knew the Lord as their Savior.
   B. Power—v. 2. The great whore had been judged. God avenged the blood of His servants at her hand.
   C. Praise—vv. 3-5
      1. People—v. 3. The Christians sang praises to God as the smoke of Babylon ascended.
      2. Praise—v. 4. The twenty-four elders continued to praise God.
      3. People—v. 5. A voice out of the throne told the small and the great to praise God.
      4. Power—v. 6. The all-powerful God reigns and all His children will reign with Him.

II. THE CLEANLINESS—vv. 7-9

A. Preparation—v. 7. The marriage supper of the Lamb is about to take place. Christ is the groom and His church (all born-again Christians) is the bride.

B. Purity—v. 8. The bride was arrayed in white, symbolizing purity. The church was made pure by the blood of Christ (I John 1:7; Isa. 1:18).

C. People—v. 9. All those in God's family (John 1:12) were invited.

III. THE COMPARISON—vv. 11-14

A. Christ—v. 11. Christ is the rider of the white horse. He is faithful and true. In righteouness He judges and makes war.

B. Characteristics—vv. 12-13. His eyes were like a flame. On His head were many crowns (King over all). He had a new name that no one knew. (See Revelation 3:12.) His blood-dipped vesture stood for full victory and triumph.

C. Control—vv. 14-16
1. Army—v. 14. All His children were in this army.
2. Allegory—v. 15. He is in control over all.
3. Almighty—v. 16. The name on His vesture and on His thigh was King of Kings and Lord of Lords.

IV. THE CONTROL—vv. 17-21

A. Supper—vv. 17-18. An invitation was given to the fowls to eat the flesh of those who opposed the Lord (cf. Zech. 14:1-9).

B. Satanic—v. 19. Satan's forces refused to give up.

C. Sentence—vv. 20-21. The beast and his followers were cast into the lake of fire, their final doom.

26
THE MILLENNIAL REIGN AND JUDGMENT
Revelation 20:1-15

I. JUSTICE FOR SATAN—vv. 1-3
    A. Angel—v. 1. An angel came down from heaven with the key to the bottomless pit.

    B. Attack—vv. 2-3. The angel bound Satan and cast him into the bottomless pit for 1,000 years. The millennial reign of Christ begins.

    There cannot be peace on earth as long as Satan is free (II Cor. 11:14; I Peter 5:8).

II. JOY FOR THE SAINTS—vv. 4-6
    A. Saints—v. 4. All who died in the Lord, who were raptured at the coming of the Lord, and who refused to worship the beast during the tribulation will reign with Christ for 1,000 years. (See Daniel 7:9-14, 25-27).

    B. Sinners—v. 5. Those who died without accepting Christ, will remain dead for 1,000 years. They will be resurrected at the end of this time to face judgment (Rev. 20:11-15).

    C. Satisfaction—v. 6. The children of God will have joy and satisfaction during these years.

III. JUDGMENT FOR SATAN—vv. 7-10
    A. Deception—vv. 7-8. Satan will be loosed for a short time. He gathered the nations, Gog and Magog, for battle (see Ezek. 38-39). Magog was the son of Japeth (Gen. 10:2). His brothers represented the northeast Kingdom. Gog was their prince (Ezek. 38:2).

B. Destruction—v. 9. God sent fire to destroy the evil people.

C. Destroyed—v. 10. Satan is cast into the lake of fire where he will be forever. Satan will no longer have any power.

IV. **JUDGMENT FOR SINNERS**—vv. 11-15

A. Place—v. 11. The great white throne judgment is different than the judgment for Christians (II Cor. 5:10). There was no place for men to hide.

B. People—vv. 12-13. The small and great stood before God and were judged according to their works. Different degrees of punishment were given.

C. Punishment—v. 14. The wicked were cast into the lake of fire. This was their final death. All Christians will have eternal life; all sinners will have eternal suffering. (See Revelation 2:11; 20:6.)

D. Personal—v. 15. "Whosoever" was not in the book was cast into hell. Take note of the "whosoever" of John 3:14-16; 4:13-14; Romans 10:13; Revelation 22:17. (See also Revelation 2:11.)

27
THE NEW JERUSALEM
Revelation 21:1-27

I. **THE CITY**—vv. 1-3

A. Place—v. 1. John saw a new heaven and new earth. The old earth was destroyed (II Peter 3:10-13).

B. Picture—v. 2. The new Jerusalem was prepared as a bride adorned for her groom.

C. People—v. 3. God is with His people and shall dwell with them forever.

II. THE COMFORT—vv. 4-7

A. Comfort—v. 4. Note the "no mores" listed here.

B. Christ—vv. 5-6. God said He made all things new. His words are faithful and true. He is the first and last. He gives the water of life.

C. Comfort—v. 7. Overcomers will inherit all things.

III. THE COMPARISON—vv. 9-22

Reverend C. M. Ward described the new Jerusalem.

The great enclosed cube is nearly 1,378 English miles every way. That is approximately the distance from Tampa, Florida, to Des Moines, Iowa, or from Dallas, Texas, to Washington, D.C. . . . Were the city to be divided into blocks as in our American cities, there would be at least 625 blocks. . . . But this unique city has another dimension. It is as high as it is wide and long. Thus following the pattern already established, and contemplating street over street and yet accommodating the highest buildings yet erected in New York, there would be at least 7,599,000 streets and 937½ billion blocks. In such a city there would be ample room for ten million houses, each large enough for 12,500 occupants measured by today's standards. At this rate the city would afford ample room for one and one-quarter quadrillion of people. That would be more than 1,000 times as many people as have been born in Adam's race up until the 1960's.

—*Pentecostal Evangel*

IV. THE CLEANLINESS—vv. 23-27

A. Peace—v. 23. There will be no darkness, since Christ is light.

B. People—v. 24. All God's children will be there, bringing honor and praise unto the Lord.
C. Peace—vv. 25-26. The gates will not be closed. There will be no night.
D. Purity—v. 27. Only the pure (made pure by salvation) will be able to enter this holy place.

28

THE NEW HEAVEN AND EARTH
Revelation 22:1-21

I. **WONDER**—vv. 1-5

Note the wonders of this new home for God's people:
A. The river of life—v. 1. (See Ezekiel 47:12.)
B. The tree of life—v. 2. (See Revelation 2:7.)
C. The curse removed—v. 3a. This is the curse from Genesis 3:1-15.
D. The throne of God—v. 2b. God's servants shall serve God and the Lamb.
E. His name on people's foreheads—v. 4
F. No night—v. 5a. God will give light. (See I John 1:5.)
G. God's people reign forever—v. 5b

II. **WORSHIP**—vv. 6-9
A. Angel—v. 6. An angel showed John the things that would soon come to pass.
B. Attention—v. 7. Christ's coming will be soon. Blessed are those, who keep His testimonies. Blessed are those who are ready.
C. Affection—vv. 8-9. John bowed before the angel in respect and honor, but the angel warned John not to bow since he was a fellow servant.

III. WARNING—vv. 10-16

A. Sacred—v. 10. Daniel was told to shut up his book (Dan. 12:9). But John was now told to keep the book open.

B. Sin—v. 11. The fulfillment of the revelation is so soon to come that men will have little time to repent. The saints are to be faithful until the end. (See Galatians 6:7-8.)

C. Savior—vv. 12-13. Christ will reward men according to their works. Christ is the first and the last—the Alpha and Omega.

D. Salvation—v. 14. Those who follow Christ will be able to enter the new Jerusalem.

E. Sin—v. 15. Sin will remain outside this city for the inside will be holy.

F. Star—v. 16. Christ is the bright and morning star (cf. Rev. 2:28).

IV. WHOSOEVER—vv. 17-19

A. Water—v. 17. This is the last invitation for salvation in the Bible. Whosoever is thirsty may drink of the water of life and be satisfied. Note that this water is free for all people. (See John 1:12; 3:16.)

B. Warning—vv. 18-19. A two-fold warning:
   1. Anyone that adds to God's Word will receive the plagues of this book. Some people add things to try to prove their doctrine.
   2. Anyone that takes away from God's Word will not have his name in the book of life and will not see the holy city. Accept His Word as it is.

C. Wonder—vv. 20-21. Christ will come quickly. His coming will be a great wonder. The benediction is found in verse 21.